Ontario Album

Ontario Album

Polar Bear Press, Toronto

First edition

Polar Bear Press

distributed by:
North 49 Books
35 Prince Andrew Place
Toronto, Ontario M3C 2H2

Canadian Cataloguing in Publication Data

Main entry under title:

Ontario Album: Images of the Past

I. Ontario – History – Pictorial Works

FC3061.0575 1998 971.3 0022 2 C98-931894-X
F1057.0575 1998

Printed in Canada

Table of Contents

Introduction

Ontario Album is just a glimpse at the wealth of information contained in other books by Terry Boyle and Ron Brown available from Polar Bear Press.

One of the marvelous benefits of publishing these books has been the pleasure of working with two such committed experts in their field. They have a passion for the fascinating subject of Ontario's past.

We had some hard choices to make, however, when it came to illustrating the books using many vintage photographs Ron and Terry have collected over the years. Some gems had to be rejected—until now.

Always agreeable and enthusiastic, Terry and Ron have opened their files and, in some cases, found more photographs for this book. Some are whimsical, some heart-rending—together they provide a true reflection of how people really lived in days gone by.

What we set out to provide is a glimpse of how people worked, shopped, travelled, vacationed and what their cities and towns looked like.

If we have made you hungry for more, we have succeeded, and you will want to know more about these fine books: *Ghost Railways of Ontario*, *Ghost Towns of Ontario: A Field Guide*, *Haunted Ontario*, *Ontario Memories*, *Toronto's Lost Villages* and *Vanished Villages*.

Polar Bear Press

The Golden Horseshoe

The Welland Canal as it appeared in the 1890s. Incorporated as a town in 1878, it had previously been called Merrittsville after William H. Merritt (see p. 12). Previous to 1842, it had been the hamlet called Aqueduct.

Niagara Falls has always proved photogenic for tourists.

The building of the Welland Canal in Fort Erie. The first canal opened in 1829 and major new construction was undertaken many times. The second canal opened in 1845, the third in 1887 and the fourth in 1932. A bypass at Welland opened in 1973.

A bell would ring at sun-up and 1,000 men would rise to labour on the Canal. One hundred teams of horses and oxen worked with the men until sundown. Progress was slow and the work was dangerous.

A source of fascination in both summer and winter, these tourists are exploring the Niagara Falls ice bridge in the 1870s. At the time of Confederation 150,000 tourists each year visited the Falls and were confronted with "the Front". This was a mile-long stretch along the riverbank full of hucksters plying their wares. In 1878, the Front was replaced by parklands and the area has been well maintained since that time.

Rodman Hall in St. Catharines was the home of William H. Merritt (1793-1862). A politician, soldier and businessman, he was the person most responsible for the original construction of the Welland Canal. This is how his home looked in 1905.

An all-female military regiment stands in front of the St. Catharine's courthouse during the 1890s.

St. Paul Street, St. Catharines, around 1905. The city has a rich history, beginning as the most heavily populated native settlement in North America prior to the arrival of white Europeans in 1790. It is now known as the "Garden City" of Canada.

The start of a circus parade on Hamilton's King Street in the late 1800s. Hamilton is a city of firsts and inventions: the flashing turn signal, the center line on highways, the first telephone exchange in the British Empire, the first pay phones in Canada, the first sulphur matches, threshing machines, sewing machines and more.

The Hamilton Farmers' Market as it looked in the late 1870s.

A workmen takes a break and looks over a procession of buggies in Gores Park, Hamilton.

The Cummer Ice and Coal wagon makes its rounds in 1895. In front of the Hamilton Yacht Club, the sign "members only admitted" is just visible.

ABOVE AND ABOVE LEFT:

Built in 1875 near Joseph Brant's home, the Brant Inn was one of Burlington's earliest tourist spots. Acres of gardens, croquet and lawn bowling greens were available. It also had a huge and beautiful ballroom. The Brant Inn remained open until the 1970s.

Bathers and boaters enjoy Sunday afternoon on the bay side of Long Beach.

An early picture of Oakville harbour.

The Sons of England (S.O.E. is on the side of the float) participate in the parade to celebrate King Edward VII's coronation in 1901. The celebrations for the coronation followed a period of deep mourning for many Canadians. Queen Victoria, Edward VII's mother, had reigned for almost 65 years and was the only monarch many Canadians had known.

In Burlington, King Edward VII's coronation was celebrated with the dedication at Brant and Water Streets of a "memorial fountain and horse trough".

Toronto

A passenger waits at the attractive Tudor-style Davenport station. It spurred the development of the hamlet and was replaced around the turn of the century by a station on the north side of St. Clair Avenue. The new station was destroyed by fire in 1997.

what do you think of little York aug 2 - 1906
picture of the crowd went to play football
how do you like. Auntie & Maggie another
little girl at alfreds Ida is all right
Good bye. George
YORK

A photograph of the York station doubled as a postcard in 1906. Removed in the 1960s, a glass GO train shelter stands on the same spot today.

This could be the stationmaster, arriving for work at the Downsview station on the Ontario Huron and Simcoe Railway. Although it carried mail and passengers, businesses did not use it. The nearby mill town of Weston got most of the trade.

The Lambton station was built by The Credit Valley Railway in the 1870s near Dundas Street and what is now Bloor Street.

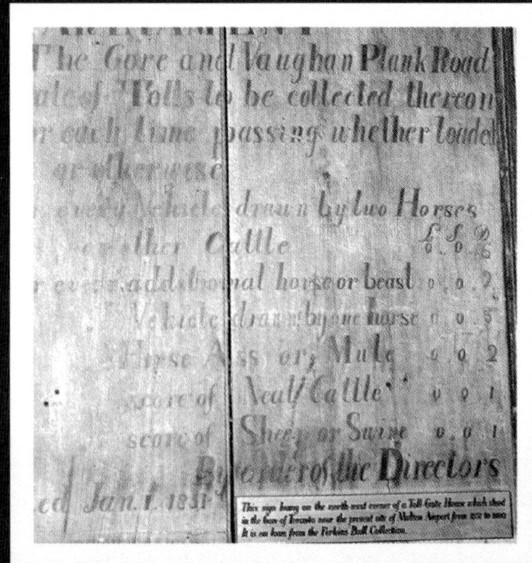

The toll-gate at Davenport Road (LEFT) and the toll sign on Gore Road (ABOVE);

"Under the Authority of Parliament. The Gore and Vaughan Plank Road rate of Tolls to be collected thereon for each time passing whether loaded or otherwise for any vehicle drawn by two horses 9d
or other cattle 2d
for every additional horse or beast 2d
vehicle drawn by one horse 3d
horse, ass or mule 2d
score of veal/cattle 1d
score of sheep or swine 1d
By order of the directors
dated Jan. 1 1851"

Hopkins General Store, Islington, near the intersection of Dundas Street and Burnhamthorpe Road has been renovated and is now home to a Chinese restaurant. Christie Biscuits provided the slate board to the left.

The Albert Britnell Book Shop, "Britnell's" to generations of book lovers, on Yonge Street north of Bloor in the 1920s. Opened in 1893, it is still run by the Britnells and has remained at the same location since

An interior view of The Albert Britnell Book Shop in the 1920s. The oldest bookstore in Ontario, it has catered to Kings, Prime Ministers, scholars, rock stars and the general public alike for over 100 years.

A view of Yonge street, looking north from Bloor in the early part of the 20th century.

Toronto Street, which runs north from King Street, one block west of Victoria, was an important financial district in 1910.

Another view of Toronto Street in 1910.

Yonge Street, around 1910, looking south from Adelaide Street.

John Oulcott's hotel near Yonge and Eglinton, which stood from 1881 until the 1930s, was on the same site as the Montgomery Tavern from which the Rebellion of 1837 was launched. The failed rebellion forced William Lyon Mackenzie into exile in the U.S. The Rebellion finally led to the Durham Report in 1841. The Oulcott Hotel also served as a post office and was eventually demolished in the 1930s.

The gracious Elliott House at Shuter and Church Streets. Virtually every type of street transportation in existence in the 20th century is depicted here, including a baby carriage.

The Queen's Hotel in Claireville opened in 1832 by John Dark is now gone. Located at the Indian Line and the Albion Plank Road, Claireville suffered when the railways bypassed it and it has gradually disappeared.

Pickering was "Duffins Creek" until the turn of the century and was established as a Quaker community in 1812. On a main stage route and near a water supply, mills were developed there. Taverns began to locate there as well and in 1856, The Grand Trunk Railway arrived. Much of the bustling pre-1900 Duffins Creek is still visible today.

Although Woodbine Avenue has changed from this dusty farm road into a wide suburban road, many of Buttonville's early buildings survive to this day.

Like many villages, it was not formally named until the post office was opened, in this case, in 1851. It had gone by the name of "Millbrook" prior to that, however, another community by that name already had a post office. The new name was chosen in honour of John Button, the first settler in the area.

Grahamsville's Magnet Hotel. Grahamsville was at the Sixth Line and Middle Road, now Steeles Avenue. The Hotel was built in 1831 and was demolished by fire fifty years later. The site is now occupied by a gas station.

The Etobicoke post office before the turn of the century. The community at what is now Dufferin Street and Eglinton Avenue started life as "Fairbanks".

ABOVE: Laurel Avenue was one of Scarborough Junction's early streets. The houses here have been replaced or surrounded by urban expansion.

Hagerman's Corners, pictured here in the late 19th century, is located in Markham at the corner of Kennedy Road and Steeles Avenue. Nicholas Hagerman was an early German settler.

The intersection of Kennedy Road and Ellesmere Avenue in the 1890s. The village of Ellesmere was on this site; the post office was in Archie Glendinning's general store.

O'Sullivan's Corners, little more than a hotel with a post office, stood at the intersection of what is now Old Sheppard Avenue and Victoria Park. The hotel was popular with diners until demolished in 1954.

The inviting interior of George Empringham's hotel at Coleman's Corners at Danforth Avenue and Dawes Road. This was the largest building in the hamlet and was later called the Danforth Hotel. It was destroyed by fire in the 1980s.

ABOVE LEFT:

The magnificent Lorne Park Hotel in Lorne Park Estates, approximately 3.2 km (2 miles) west of Oakville. A fabulous "pleasure ground" for the wealthy, it was beset by financial woes and the hotel burned to the ground in 1920.

LEFT:

The Scarborough Beach just after the turn of the century. Built of wood, many of the walkways and other structures have not survived.

ABOVE:

On the banks of the Rouge River, the Rosebank House was a popular summer retreat for folks from West Hill and Pickering.

ABOVE RIGHT:

Boaters and spectators enjoy the Toronto Canoe Club on Lake Ontario, early 1900s.

RIGHT:

The C.N.E. crowd gathers around a bandshell in 1910. The buildings in the background were: Provinces, Administration, Art Gallery, Railway Exhibits and Applied Arts.

ABOVE:

The ferry *Bluebell* crossing Toronto Bay to Hanlan's Point. The passengers may have been on their way to see the Toronto Maple Leafs baseball team play a game on the diamond there.

ABOVE LEFT:

Toronto Island Park at the turn of the century, showing the Lagoon and a bridge in the background.

LEFT:

In Mimico, an early streetcar takes businessmen to their daily labour.

Toronto Island provided a variety of water sport activity on Sunday afternoons in the early 1900s.

ABOVE: McMaster University on Bloor Street West at the turn of the century, now the Royal Conservatory of Music.

In 1910, this was the Hospital for Sick Children. Located on College Street just west of Bay Street, it is now owned by the Red Cross. It was here that pablum was developed, the polio epidemic was fought and the first milk pasteurization plant in Canada was installed. Elizabeth McMaster was instrumental in opening the hospital in 1875.

Yonge Street, looking north from King Street, in the early 1900s.

The King Edward Hotel on King Street east of Yonge, as it appeared after the turn of the century. Common on many landmark photographs, details were added by an artist.

The Arlington Hotel graced the corner of King Street and John Street in the early 1900s. Part of "New Town", this area housed parliament buildings at King and Simcoe Streets and Upper Canada College and Government House until 1900.

The Telegram building at the corner of Bay Street and Melinda Street. John Ross Robertson, publisher of the Evening Telegram, was also chairman of the Hospital for Sick Children and spearheaded its move to larger quarters at Elizabeth and College Streets in 1891.

The northwest corner of Yonge and Temperance Streets circa 1905.

Spadina Avenue, looking north from Queen Street in the early 1900s. Knox College is in the distance.

Yonge Street, looking north from just south of Temperance Street, early 1900s.

This stone mine was at the Forks of the Credit circa 1895. It is difficult to make out where the winch supporting the stone block is located—certainly not 'round the worker's neck, as this camera angle suggests!

Burnhamthorpe Village at the intersection of Burnhamthorpe and Dixie Roads. Close by was the tavern and hamlet called "Puckey Huddle". Only the church, dating back to the 1840s, remains.

The Brittannia Church, built in 1843, still stands. It replaced a log church built in 1830. Now it is surrounded by a gas station, burger bar, donut shop and six lanes of traffic on Highway 10.

ABOVE:

Thistletown retained many of its early hamlet buildings even into the 1950s. None of these structures at Islington Avenue and Albion Road have survived.

ABOVE LEFT:

The general store in historic Cookstown where the railway station still survives as a remodelled store.

Main Street West, Meadowvale, one of Ontario's best-preserved areas where many historic and grand old buildings remain intact

Eastern Ontario

The gentlemen farmers of Whitby pose with a new model steam tractor. This impressive-looking engine made by the Waterloo Manufacturing Co. was probably made in the 1870s.

The Commercial House in Cobourg in the 1870s. A popular hotel and saloon combination, these establishments were segregated between "Men's" drinking parlours and "Women & Escorts only" parlours, for the next 100 years. Appropriately, a pair of designated drivers are on standby.

Whitby in the 1860s had two competing hotels, "The Ontario" and "The Royal". The No. 4 Furniture Company did a thriving business and no doubt its wares have fueled many an antiques dealer over the years. The hand-painted wagon in the foreground laden with sacks of flour appears to be leaving William Donaldson Flour, Grains and Provisions.

Port Hope enjoying a summer celebration circa 1880. Notice the many miniature Union Jacks festooning the buildings on the left. The banner over the street proclaims "Beware How You Tread On His Tail".

The Midland Railway Roundhouse in Port Hope was built in the 1860s. This railway was a response to neighbouring Cobourg's line to Peterborough. The "Midland" railway ran from Port Hope to Lindsay, Orillia and Midland. While a branch line was eventually built through Peterborough to Lakefield, the entire line was taken over by the Grand Trunk Railway in the late 1880s.

A view of Port Hope in the 1860s. Port Hope today has kept much of its 19th century charm intact.

The prosperous "Benson House" in Lindsay. Taken in 1892, the establishment combined the J. P. Ryley Saloon and a two-storey hotel. The sturdy stagecoach out front represents the state-of-the-art town transportation.

The main street of Lindsay hosts a parade in the early part of the 20th century. Several figures are blurred because photographic processes at the time required subjects to remain still for several seconds or more in order for the image to be clear.

The ice-storm of 1998 in Eastern Ontario and Quebec had a few predecessors, as this ice jam in Belleville in 1884 proves.

ABOVE: Bowmanville in the 1890s at the intersection of King and Temperance Streets. The Town Hall is over the stores on the left. The town's bandstand is situated opposite the Fire Hall. "Miss A. Medland's Corner Store" graces the corner building on the right.

LEFT: Marlbank Cement Works on the Bay of Quinte Railway Line in 1899. Part of Edward Rathburn's turn-of-the-century industrial empire, little remains of his vast holdings and enterprises. In 1910, the Bay of Quinte Railway was absorbed by the Canadian Northern Railway in its attempt to complete a main line from Toronto to Ottawa.

The Blackstock main street in the early 1900s. The Post Office is on the right and William Cowan's General Store is on the left.

Madoc was once the jumping-off point for the gold fields near Hastings. The Grand Junction Railway carried passengers until the late 1950s. The Station was later neglected, vandalized and finally burned in 1990.

Bancroft House during Bancroft's mining boom was so popular a destination that it had its own coach for transporting guests.

A crowd gathered in Kingston's Market Square on July 1, 1867 to hear the proclamation announcing Confederation.

Kingston Farmers' Market

Bedford Mills, just north of Kingston, shows off its sawmill, grist mill, church and hillside estates.

Mill Street in Carleton Place circa 1889. This bustling milltown southwest of Ottawa displays a steady traffic of horse-drawn wagons to its textile mills.

The corner of Rideau and Sussex in Ottawa in 1865. The wide wooden sidewalks, stagecoaches and hoop dress of the woman in the midground give the distinct impression of a wild west tableau—not the new staid national capital. Known as a "lumber" town, Queen Victoria's choice of Ottawa as the nation's capital was controversial.

Southwestern Ontario

The flood in March of 1913 provided some water fun on Canal Street in Dunnville.

In Brampton, the train station was located next to the undertaker's.

The main street of Brampton as it appeared in the early part of the century. Although traffic was light, parking was at a premium.

Guelph, the Royal City, decorated by J.J. Turner's Sons of Peterboro, for what may be a July 1st celebration in the early 1900's.

Three Guelph hoteliers in 1895. Left to right they are: Dave Martin, Wellington Hotel; Folk John Henderson, Royal Hotel; Lot Singular, Victoria Hotel.

Guelph in 1875 looked like a town in the Old West, except for the brick church in the background. Part of Wellington County, there is a sign for the Wellington Hotel and the Wellington Boot and Shoe Manufacturing establishment. Day's Bookstore, alas, no longer exists.

A typical church outing at the Elora Gorge around 1900.

Employees of the Guelph Railway—the streetcars. May we have your ticket, please?

Fording the Elora Gorge has always been fun.

An early view of Fergus' main street. Mr. Fitzpatrick, the Harness Maker, stands outside his establishment on the left.

The Fergus Railway Station and Telephone Office in the early days.

Fergus in 1895. A windmill is visible on the right. Scottish stonemasons constructed some 200 buildings here in the 19th century that still stand.

This is how the main street of Kitchener was rebuilt. Notice the street-car on the tracks at left. A large German settlement, the town was called Berlin at this time. During World War I the name was changed to honour Lord Horatio H. Kitchener.

A bread delivery truck in Kitchener in the early 1900s. "Canada Bread the Best" is on the side of the coach.

Acton's Church Street, under construction, with the Happy Thought Ranges store on the right. These stoves graced the kitchens of many homes throughout southwestern Ontario.

The Acton Fire Department parade, ironically, in front of Happy Thought Ranges.

The hardware store in St. Jacobs as it looked around 1900. Named for a Mennonite farmer, it was originally called "Jakobstettle" or Jacob's village.

Milton's main street in 1905. Originally called Martin's Mills in 1837, the population of 100 changed the name, either in honour of the poet John Milton or as a corruption of Milltown.

An inn in Waterloo where travellers, including the stagecoach, stopped for refreshments and sometimes lodging. Goods were also transported this way. The man, and especially the boy on the left, are obviously pleased with the packages they have just received.

The luxurious Caledonia Hotel at Caledonia Springs in September of 1875 was a meeting place for the rich and powerful. The gentleman fourth from the left has just expelled pipe smoke, creating a halo effect.

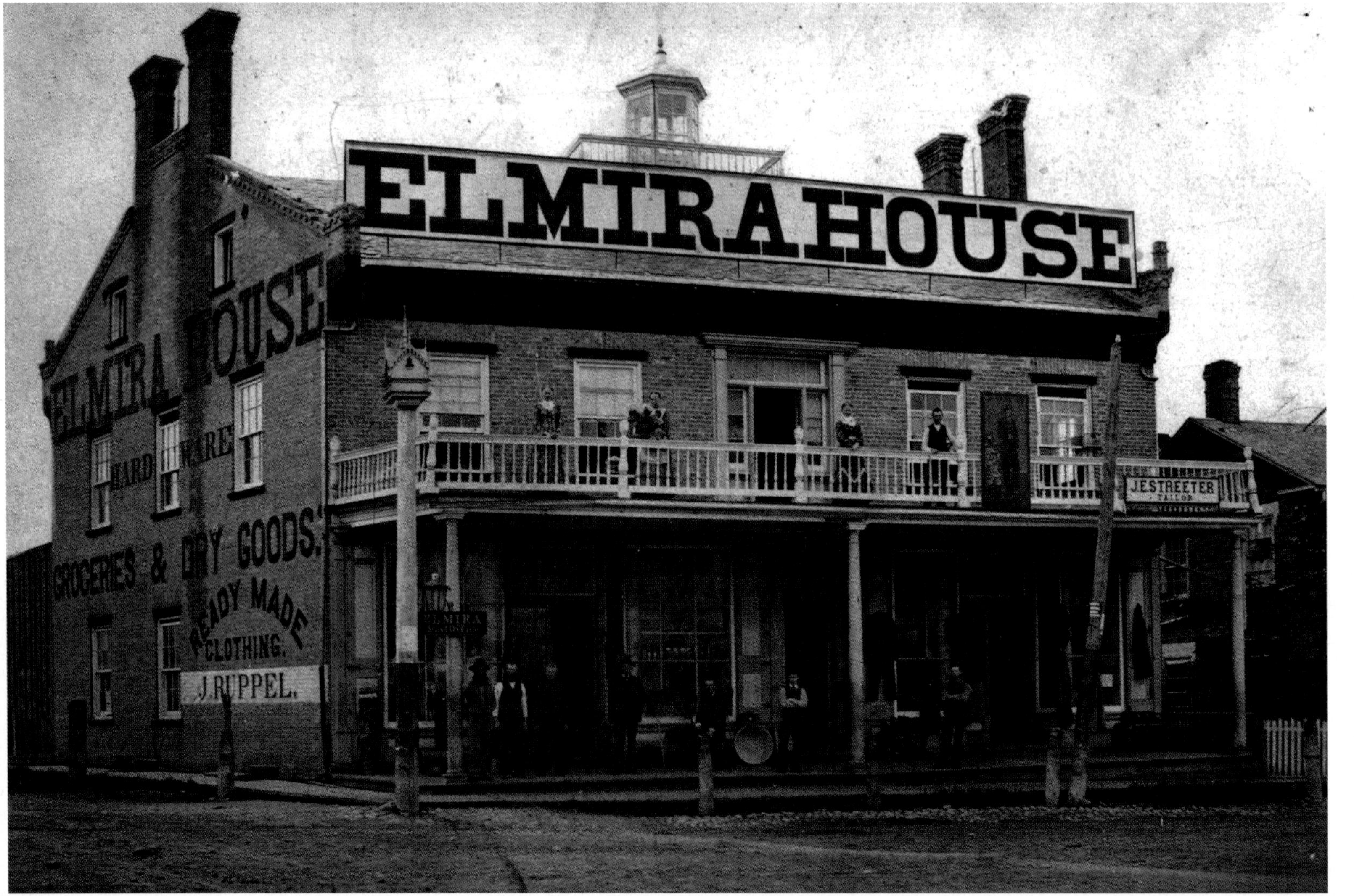

The Elmira House and Post Office was a hub of activity. Built in 1860, this picture was probably taken shortly thereafter.

The damaged photo depicts the Woodstock militia on the main street in 1860. The sign on the left is for a carriage factory.

The age of this photo is evident because of the wooden sidewalk. Otherwise this scene could be witnessed today in the area around Waterloo. The Mennonite community in southwestern Ontario eschews motors and, depending upon their degree of orthodoxy, electricity as well. Buggies are still manufac-

The chocolate dipping department at McCormick's Candy Factory in London around 1916.

An omnibus near Victoria Park in London sets out on a tour in 1901.

The Children's Aid Excursion raised funds for orphaned and homeless children. This railway car travelled in the London, Dundas, Mt. Hope area.

The beach on Lake Huron at Kincardine around 1900.

The beach at Kincardine around 1900. The girls aren't too shy to lift their skirts and paddle while a boy in a lifejacket looks on.

Sunbathing on the beach at Grand Bend in the 1930s. Was it the lack of sunscreen that kept so many on the shaded balcony?

Two views of the Kincardine waterfront around 1900. An important port on the shores of Lake Huron, the marina now is used by fishermen and other pleasure boaters.

A beach guest house at Grand Bend was typical of its kind in the early part of the 20th century. This was taken in the 1930s. Guests' cars were parked at the front and what looks like a tour bus is at the far left.

Grand Bend's main street in 1900.

Grand Bend has its first school fair in 1921. Five schools participated and all the children were in the parade down main street.

The beach just south of Southampton, near Port Elgin, before 1900. Chantry Island and the lighthouse are just barely visible on the left.

Part of downtown Goderich before 1900.

The salt mill in Goderich before World War I.

The canal at Long Beach, with the lighthouse in the background, was an ideal place for a Sunday stroll around 1900. The man on the left is holding what is probably the camera case.

The fabulous New Balmoral Hotel, advertised in New York City, was to be the centrepiece of St. Joseph in 1904. It was built by the ambitious Narcisse Cantin who convinced French Canadians from Michigan, among others, to settle in St. Joseph. The outbreak of the First World War dashed his hopes and although the hotel stood until 1928, it never opened.

Family and friends gather at the Reid cottage on Long Beach, August 13, 1900.

Fort Malden, near Amherstburg, as it looked in 1895. This military settlement was named for Lord Jeffery Amherst, Governor-General of British North America from 1760 to 1763.

These young boys pause from their labour on a dirt street in Amherstburg.

Although clearing snow from the tracks was a common scene everywhere, this photo was taken in Flesherton.

A photographer sets up a shot at the marina in Amherstburg.

Clinton's main street, just prior to 1900. Clinton was known for its thriving newspapers and a piano factory. Both Timothy Findley and Alice Munro, who has lived in Clinton for many years, included the factory in their novels.

A home in Cambridge, around 1900, shared by four generations.

The community of Blair, just northwest of Cambridge, came out in full force to repair the track—and pose for a picture.

Young Chinese immigrants, sporting new straw boaters, arrive in Sarnia via the Tunnel in the early 1900s.

A typical general store. When purchased items were not put in a box the wrapping paper and string, next to the glass case, were used. "Paper or plastic?" was unheard of in those days.

A dockside, railside view of Sarnia around 1900.

The main street of Brussels, around 1900.

Peddlars travelled from town to town and homestead to homestead to sell dry goods. This one carries some goods from Wingham and is selling to a housewife in Queenston.

Sarnia's waterfront in the early 1900s. Sarnia began life as a fur trading post called The Rapids.

Listowel's main street in 1873 was the site of major construction when the bridge was built.

Georgian Bay

The Canada House Hotel in Penetanguishene circa 1890. At the time the town was at the centre of the lumbering boom and had four major mills in operation.

The Penetanguishene Hotel in 1898; it offered the finest in luxury accommodation and was dedicated to attracting "the annual patronage of the best class of people". The famous aviators, Orville & Wilbur Wright vacationed here. It burned to the ground, sadly, during WW I

Penetanguishene "Place of the White Rolling Sands" in the late 1930s. Main Street leads down to the waters of Georgian Bay.

C. E. Wright and his employees pose next to his butcher shop in Penetanguishene in the late 1890s. Carcasses are on display as are his two fine buckboards, presumably used for delivery.

James Street in Parry Sound in October, 1910. Wesley's Confectionary and W. Went Gents Furnishings are on the right.

ABOVE: Posing for pictures on the farm in the 1940s near Parry Sound.

LEFT: Collecting sap to make maple syrup on the Richmond's farm in Carling Township in the 1940s.

A Sunday afternoon picnic near Simcoe around the turn of the century. Baked beans, cakes and preserves in sealers are on the menu. Everyone has a cloth napkin.

Cruise boats like this one were popular throughout Georgian Bay.

Fishing smacks jockey for space in the confines of Bustards Islands prior to 1900.

A car is moved off Franklin Island in the 1920s and onto Sylvestor Richmond's sailboat

A view of the Barrie harbour with the market building on the right. The house on the left also features ornamental iron-work on its roof, fashionable at the time.

The Barrie Market Building at Mulcaster and Collier Streets after it was renovated in 1877. It has been drastically renovated since, the ornamental roofwork and towers have disappeared. This two-storey building is now the three-storey City Hall.

Dunlop and Owen Streets in Barrie after the devastating fire in June 1875.

The steamer *Asia* was built in St. Catharines in 1873. On September 14, 1882, laden with 85 tons (39 tonnes) of cargo, crew, passengers and 15 horses, it sank. Only two people survived to tell the tragic story. Two days later they reached land where local Native people found them and took them the 25 miles (40 km) to Parry Sound.

The steamer *Magnolia* is tied up at the Midland wharf.

A fishing fleet in Collingwood Harbour in the 1880s. It was originally known as Hen-and-Chickens Harbour because there was one large and four small islands that have since become part of the mainland.

The Northern Railway Station at Barrie in the 1870s with the paddlewheel boat *Lady of the Lakes* in the background and two buckboards in the foreground. Three popular choices of transportation and no queues for any of them!

The Fire Department is charging to the rescue on Owen Sound's main street in front of the Grey & Bruce Loan Company.

Looking north up Syke Street, downtown Meaford late 1800s. In 1880 there were eight hotels, two grist mills, two sawmills, two tanners, two woollen mills, a foundry, a machine shop and a variety of other shops on Syke Street. Fire and flood destroyed much of Old Meaford.

Gravenhurst's main street in the late 1800s.

The iceman cometh—to Collingwood in 1875. William Swain was the "ice dealer" and he is stopped in front of Telfer Bros. Bakery and Archer & Fluent Feed. His helper is holding a block of ice in the huge tongs that were used especially for this purpose.

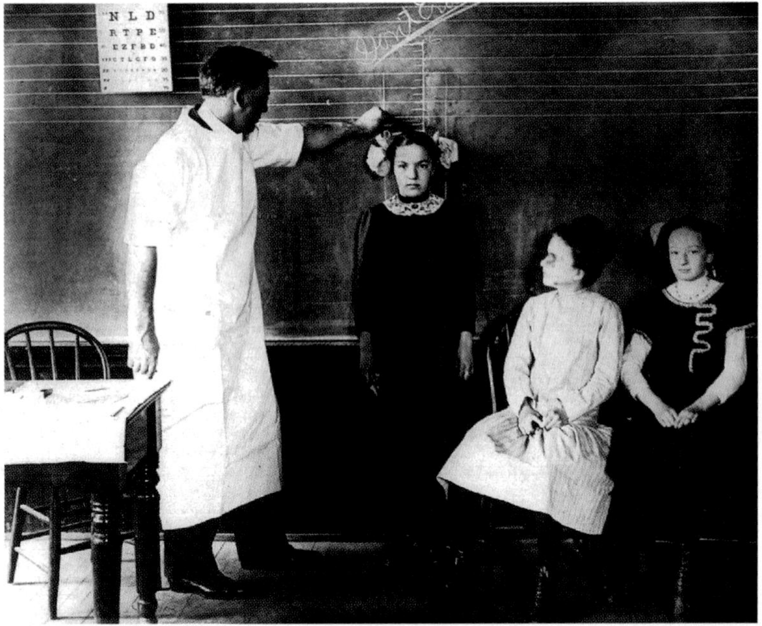

Often the only healthcare was provided by one doctor. Here he pays a school visit in Chatsworth.

Here two young patients visit the doctor in his office and bravely face the prospect of an injection.

The beautiful Capstan Inn at Wasaga Beach in 1939.

The *Jane Miller*, a Wiarton ship built in 1879, set out on November 25, 1881 from Owen Sound. Just two miles from its final destination, horrified onlookers saw its lights go out. Carrying passengers, crew and freight, no survivors were found.

Reid and Ayling's *Trail of the Caribou* on the ground at Wasaga Beach. They flew from there to London, England in August of 1934 for a total of 3,100 miles (5,900 km) in 34 hours and 55 minutes. Adverse weather and a fuel shortage forced them down; their destination had been Baghdad.

In 1940 Wasaga Beach was a popular tourist spot. Soldiers from nearby Camp Borden came to Wasaga Beach on weekends during World War II. Crowds of 100,000 were not unusual and became even larger after the war.

Northern Ontario

Port Arthur inaugurates its Electric Street Railway in March of 1892. Toques, fedoras, bowlers and caps all share in the headware of the day.

A view of Port Arthur Harbour from the C.P.R. steamer *Alberta* in 1884. The wharves supported a number of covered sections that helped shelter the dockhandlers and horses from the elements.

CNR's Driftwood Station, just west of Cochrane in 1920. Perhaps the gentlemen and their faithful companion on the railway "jigger" were on their way to Cochrane for some civilized recreation. The family on the platform appear to have been painting and plastering, perhaps the very

A lovely homestead on the Muskoka River. Although the original photo credits do not say if it is the north or south branch, the rocky terrain in the background is softened by the gentle poplars in the foreground. The craftsmanship of the rocking chair on the porch is exquisite.

Sauble Beach on the Bruce Peninsula was a thriving mill town near the turn of the century. Here the mill pond is shown with one of the sturdy little tugboats that manoeuvre the logs to shore.

Loggers at Sauble Beach take a break from their dangerous work. Taken around 1880, some of these workers were 16 and under—having started their working lives as their teens had just begun.

Some dapper looking loggers on their "alligator boat" in 1890. This shallow draft paddle wheeler was partially amphibious and easily negotiated beaches where logs had drifted ashore.

A spectacular shot of an unknown lumber mill in the 1880s. This incredibly rough terrain is criss-crossed by small railways manned by loggers pushing carts.

In the boomtowns of northern Ontario at the turn of the century, hotels such as the "Lake View" at O'Brien's Landing were hastily constructed to ensure accommodation for the newly arriving miners.

Miners set out for their shift. These spartan shanty-towns with their basic electrical service were "home" for these workers for months at a

A logging depot at an unknown location in Ontario's northland circa 1880. A rather dapper pair of gentlemen share a business consultation with a heavily bearded engineer in his work duds. Notice the heavy-duty lantern light on the engine that was the state-of-the-art in illumination technology at the time.

These "well-balanced"lumbermen load up their flatbed rail cars with the day's haul.

The main street of Cobalt in the late 1800s was hastily-erected during the silver mining boom.

Cobalt, near the shores of Lake Temiskaming, was the silver mining boom town of the north. The first prospectors came to the area in the 1880s and by 1908 it became internationally known by the sheer size and density of the silver veins there. One of the early arrivals provided a liquid priority for the thirsty prospectors.

Members of a legislative tour visited the Mine Centre Hotel in June of 1899 (right). The hotel was the scene of many a boisterous, rollicking time for the miners. The hotel, also the scene for regattas, was barged downstream to Fort Frances after the gold rush ended in the early 1900s.

The Mine Centre Hotel and the steamer Majestic on the same day as the photo below. Just east of Rainy Lake on the Seine River, Mine Centre was the hub of the frenzied gold fever that hit Northwestern Ontario in the late 1800s.

This shot of Biscotasing railway station in the 1920s shows part of a baseball game in progress. The town developed into a sawmill town that had two churches, a school, the accompanying Hudson's Bay Store and a competing general store. A young clerk from Eaton's in Toronto briefly settled here, and later changed his name to Chief Grey Owl.

This Hudson's Bay Company store in Biscotasing (north of Sudbury) circa 1915 makes this settlement appear rather sedate and civilized. Founded in 1880 as a CPR construction town, Biscotasing had one of the highest per capita concentration of bars and brothels in the north.

The Cochrane theatre as it looked in the 1920s. It is still there today.

The partnership of Scott, Scott and MacGregor hang their legal shingle on the Main Street of Latchford (near Cobalt) in the 1870s. Their business neighbours are Jack Hong Laundry and, of course, the popular Prospectors "Supplies" Store.

W.J. Parsons set up his "American Fair" Dry Goods store in 1887 in North Bay. His sign proclaimed "EVERYTHING SOLD HERE AT ROCK BOTTOM PRICES". The times may change but the business ethos remains strikingly contemporary.

Silver Mountain Mine in June of 1899. This prosperous and rough-hewn mining community near the Ontario-Minnesota border is presided over by some of the founding fathers at its summer picnic.

The Port Arthur Duluth and Western Railway that serviced this community was created, in part, by the growing rivalry between Port Arthur and Fort William to become a main terminus for the Canadian

An enterprising logger hires some local talent to provide muscle for his winter operations near North Bay circa 1900.

Winter clearing operations for a new settlement. The skill involved in this painstaking operation would take no small amount of brawn, determination and teamwork.

The New Windsor Hotel in Bala accommodated vacationers to the Muskoka area in the early 1900s. Weekends would see an influx of Torontonians who had headed north to take in the fresh air and clear water. The ferry in the background is typical of those that plied the Muskoka Lakes on their journeys from Gravenhurst, Bala, Bracebridge and Port Carling.

Bala Railway Station in August of 1916. A sultry summer eve sees a group in their summer whites take their ease while waiting for the trip back to Hogtown. As better highways were built to service "cottage country" north of Toronto, week-end passenger service by both the CPR and CNR was phased out after WWII. This particular station was dismantled in the 1970s.

The streetcar in New Liskeard made a stop at the ice cream factory in 1916.

The spring flood at South Porcupine in 1922 made it necessary to shop by canoe and meet the train by canoe.

This ramshackle settlement on the shores of Lake Temiskaming in 1890 was the first village of Silver Centre. It rivaled Cobalt in silver production for a time but was later moved from the original townsite closer to the mine proper.

Silver Centre's hotel, left, and mine office formed the meeting place of this boisterous boom town. One could imagine the interesting wagers and bets placed here on payday.

On the north shore of Lake Superior, Jackfish was first settled by Scandinavians not quite ready to give up the Nordic landscape.

Later in the 1880s the CPR chose it for their coal dock and it became a more diverse and bustling little port.

The Scandinavian fisherman of Jackfish continued to fish while the CPR went about linking their routes with the growing number of smaller northern rail lines.

Depot Harbour on the shores of Georgian Bay in the early 1900s. The sport of ice sailing took hold until the blades could be put away in favour of those other boats with keels.

Barnet's Brule Lake boarding house in the 1920s. At the western edge of what is now Algonquin Park, this large structure would have had a fabulous view of the surrounding countryside. With this many inhabitants, however, the soundscape may not have been as pleasant.

Silver Islet's windswept shore sports a rough wharf and covered motor-launch. This launch no doubt acted as a ferry for the miners' daily trips back and forth from their village to their considerably damper mine.

Silver Islet near Thunder Bay. This was the site of one of the richest silver mines in North America during the 1870s and 80s. Perhaps the gentleman in the foreground is one William Frue, an engineer who took several attempts to shore up a breakwater sturdy enough to sink the mine shaft. Alas, Lake Superior was to prove too harsh a tenant and flooded it in 1883.

French River's rocky character belies its existence as Georgian Bay's hardest-working lumber town in the late 1880s.

Sawmill employees of Spragge, near the shores of Lake Huron, take a break in the early 1900s. Perhaps they are looking at the fine lines of the schooners entering the bay, as is the lady on her veranda in the upper right.

In the heart of Algonquin Park, the defunct Gilmour Mills logging concern was turned into a tourist resort. Mowat Lodge was probably the location of artist Tom Thomson's last civilized meal, as he was tragically drowned while he was a guest there.

The Nipissing Central Railway operated one of the first elevated streetcar tracks in the early 1900s. This system helped shunt miners between Cobalt, Kerr Lake and Silver Centre.

About our Authors

Terry Boyle

Terry Boyle is the author of ONTARIO MEMORIES and is also a popular radio broadcaster. He has talked and written about Ontario culture, folklore and history for more than 20 years and is a recognized authority. He has been an art gallery curator, poet, gardening expert and is a special education teacher. He lives near Parry Sound, Ontario.

Ron Brown

Ron Brown is Ontario's foremost ghost town expert and has been writing and lecturing about Canada's changing historical landscape for over 30 years. A geographer and town planner by trade, he scouts unusual locations for film companies and conducts tours to ghost towns and historical landscapes. He is a regular guest on CBC radio and is an award-winning writer.

Index

Photo Credits

p.9 Ontario Archives ACC16856-17974
National Archives of Canada PA145426
From the collection of Terry Boyle
From the collection of Ron Brown
p.10 National Archives of Canada PA145426
p.11 Ontario Archives ACC9140-S13312 (Niagara Falls)
Ontario Archives ACC2331-S4214 (Fort Erie)
Ontario Archives ACC6287-S8247 (Fort George)
p.12 Ontario Archives ACC14054-12 (Rodman Hall)
Ontario Archives ACC6847-S4821 (Courthouse)
Ontario Archives ACC16856-17974 (Niagara Falls)
p.13 Ontario Archives ACC14054-44 (St. Paul Street)
Ontario Archives ACC2130-53232 (Long Beach)
p.14 Ontario Archives ACC2519-S11930 (Circus Parade)
p.15 Ontario Archives ACC14032-130 (Cummer Ice)
Ontario Archives ACC2728-ST117 (Gores Park)
Ontario Archives ACC2728-ST110 (Farmer's Market)
p.16 Ontario Archives ACC9379-S14995 (Brant Hotel)
Ontario Archives ACC9355-S14712 (Lawn Bowling)
p.17 Ontario Archives ACC9209-S13577 (Oakville)
p.18 Ontario Archives ACC9355-S14711 (Burlington)
p.19 Ontario Archives ACC9355-S14710 (Burlington Memorial)
p.20 Ontario Archives PA179542 (Davenport)
p.21 Paterson George Collection (Downsview)
p.22 CP Archives A-21040 (Lambton)
Ontario Archives 3932 (Toll Sign)
p.23 From the Collection of Ron Brown
p.24 Britnell's
p.25 From the Collection of Terry Boyle
p.26 From the Collection of Terry Boyle
p.27 From the Collection of Terry Boyle
p.28 Metropolitan Toronto Reference Library,
Salmon Collection (Queen's Hotel)
From the Collection of Terry Boyle (Elliot House)
City of Toronto Archives James 7277 (Oulcott Hotel)
p.29 From the Collection of Terry Boyle
p.30 From the Collection of Ron Brown
p.31 From the Collection of Ron Brown
p.32 From the Collection of Ron Brown
p.33 From the Collection of Ron Brown

p.34 Lytle Collection N292.6 (Lorne Park)
Met. Toronto Reference Library T11008 (Coleman's Corners)
From the Collection of Terry Boyle (Scarborough Beach)
p.35 From the Collection of Ron Brown (Rosebank)
From the Collection of Terry Boyle (C.N.E.)
From the Collection of Terry Boyle (Toronto Canoe Club)
p.36-9 From the Collection of Terry Boyle
p.46 From the Collection of Terry Boyle
p.47 National Archives PA147737 (Commercial House)
From the Collection of Terry Boyle (Whitby)
p.48 Ontario Archives ACC14054-17 (Port Hope)
National Archives C23250 (Roundhouse)
p.49 National Archives C38427 (Port Hope)
p.50 From the Collection of Terry Boyle
p.51 From the Collection of Terry Boyle
p.52 Ontario Archives ACC13781-160 (Belleville)
p.53 Lennox & Addington County Museum N-3953 (Marlbank)
p.54 Ontario Archives ACC9413-S14895 (Blackstock)
Ontario Archives ACC9334-S14827 (Madoc)
p.55 Ontario Archives ACC6493-S11302 (Bancroft)
p.56 Queen's University Archives (Market Square)
Kingston Historical Society (Farmer's Market)
p.57 From the Collection of Terry Boyle (Prince George Hotel)
p.58 National Archives C1345 (Carleton Place)
p.59 National Archives C494 (Ottawa)
p.62 Ontario Archives ACC9707 S16335
p.63 Ontario Archives ACC15107-40 (Train Station)
Ontario Archives ACC16856 S15180 (Brampton)
p.64 Ontario Archives ACC2398 S5466 (Hoteliers)
Ontario Archives ACC9339-N83 (Guelph)
p.65 Ontario Archives ACC9347 S14589
p.66 Wellington County Museum Archives PH1187
p.67 Wellington County Museum Archives PH6321
Ontario Archives ACC2398 S5461 (Guelph Railway Employees)
p.68 Ontario Archives ACC4563 S6574 (Main Street)
Ontario Archives ACC 11056-29 (Train Station)
Ontario Archives ACC4563 S6583 (Fergus)
p. 69 From the Collection of Terry Boyle
p.70 Ontario Archives ACC9339 N23 (Church Street)
Ontario Archives ACC9339 N14 (Fire Department)
p.71 From the Collection of Terry Boyle (St. Jacobs)
National Archives PA60934 (Milton)
p.72 From the Collection of Terry Boyle
p.73 National Archives PA59235
p.74 From the Collection of Terry Boyle
p.75 Ontario Archives ACC12826-6 (Woodstock)
Ontario Archives ACC6355 S9836 (Waterloo)
p.76 From the Collection of Terry Boyle
p.77 From the Collection of Terry Boyle
p.78 From the Collection of Terry Boyle (Top left)
Ontario Archives ACC6271 S8093 (Top right)
Ontario Archives ACC9681 S15568 (Bottom)
p.79 Ontario Archives
p.80 Ontario Archives ACC9681 S15560
p.81 Ontario Archives ACC9681 S15559 (Top left)
Ontario Archives ACC9681 S15563 (Top right)
Ontario Archives A0265 (Bottom right)
p.82 Ontario Archives ACC4822 S4747
p.83 Ontario Archives ACC13544-9
p.84 From the Collection of Terry Boyle
p.85 Ontario Archives ACC14032-52
p.86 Ontario Archives ACC2537 S11993 (Top left)

Ontario Archives ACC6906 S13523 (Top right)
Ontario Archives ACC16856 2652 (Bottom right)
p.90 Ontario Archives ACC6271 S8065 (Queenston)
Ontario Archives ACC6520 S15580 (Brussels)
p.91 Ontario Archives ACC13563-14
p.94 Ontario Archives ACC2375-S5374 (Canada House)
National Archives PA163909 (Hotel)
p.95 Ontario Archives ACC2375-S5365 (C.E. Butcher)
Ontario Archives ACC14719-36 (Penetanguishene)
p.96 National Archives PA16630 (Parry Sound)
p.97 From the Collection of Terry Boyle
p.98 Ontario Archives A0204 (Picnic)
Ontario Archives ACC6355-S9644 (Victoria)
p.99 From the Collection of Terry Boyle
p.100 Ontario Archives S-17901B
p.101 From the Collection of Terry Boyle
p.102 Ontario Archives ACC9082-313061 (*Asia*)
Ontario Archives ACC2375-S5384 (*Magnolia*)
From the Collection of Terry Boyle (Collingwood)
p.103 Ontario Archives
p.,104 Ontario Archives
p.105 Ontario Archives ACC2203-S3671 (Gravenhurst)
Ontario Archives ACC13045-15 (Meaford)
From the Collection of Terry Boyle (Collingwood)
p.106 Ontario Archives S15514 (School)
Ontario Archives ACC14506-3 (Visit)
p.107 Ontario Archives ACC14719-14 (Capstan Inn)
Ontario Archives ACC14996-3 (*Jane Miller*)
p.108 From the Collection of Terry Boyle
p.109 Ontario Archives ACC14719-42 (Wasaga Beach)
p.112 Thunder Bay Museum
p.113 Ontario Northland Transportation Commission (Driftwood)
p.114 Ontario Archives A0267 (Sauble Beach)
Ontario Archives A0266 (Alligator Point)
Ontario Archives ACC2271-S5196 (Port Stanley)
p.115 National Archives PA C34346
p.116 Ontario Ministry of Natural Resources
p.117 From the Collection of Ron Brown
p.118 Ontario Archives ACC16378-16
p.119 From the Collection of Ron Brown
p.120 Ontario Archives ACC6995-S14555 (Biscotasing)
Ontario Ministry of Natural Resources (Biscotasing Store)
p.121 Ontario Archives ACC9160-S13796 (Cochrane)
From the Collection of Ron Brown (Latchford)
p.122 Ontario Archives S18083 (American Bay)
Ontario Archives ACC10399-6 (Silver Mountain)
p.123 From the Collection of Terry Boyle
Ontario Archives ACC11778-S16941 (Clearing the forest)
Collection of Isabelle Thomson (Playing the fields)
p.124 National Archives PA32248 (New Windsor Hotel)
p.125 National Archives PA69792 (Bala Station)
p.126 From the Collection of Terry Boyle
p.127 From the Collection of Terry Boyle
p.128 From the Collection of Ron Brown
p.129 National Archives PA32450
p.130 From the Collection of Ron Brown
p.131 From the Collection of Ron Brown
p.132 From the Collection of Ron Brown
p.133 From the Collection of Ron Brown